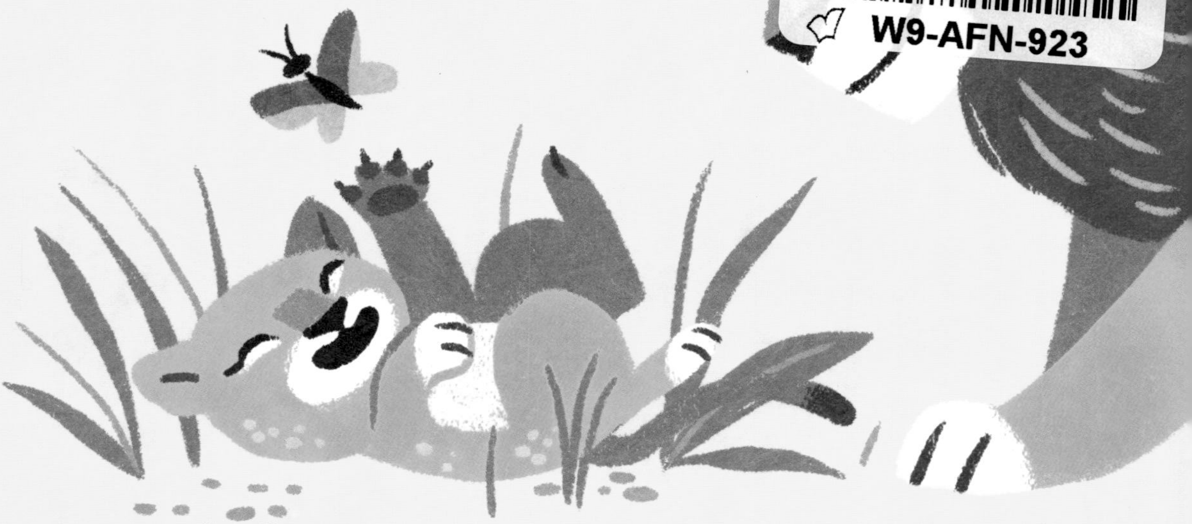

Uh-oh, baby.
What a mess.
Time for a bath!

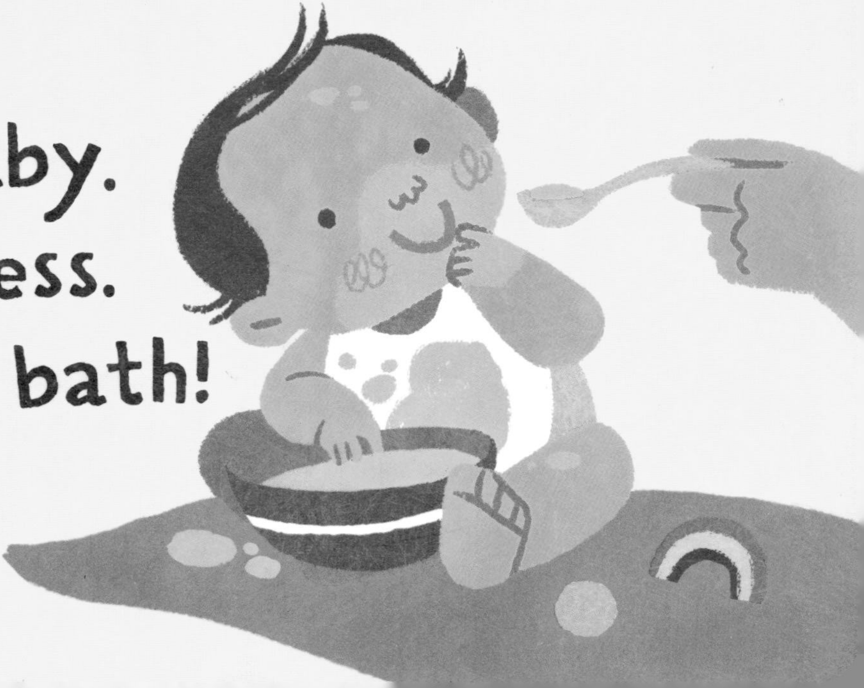

Elephants splash.

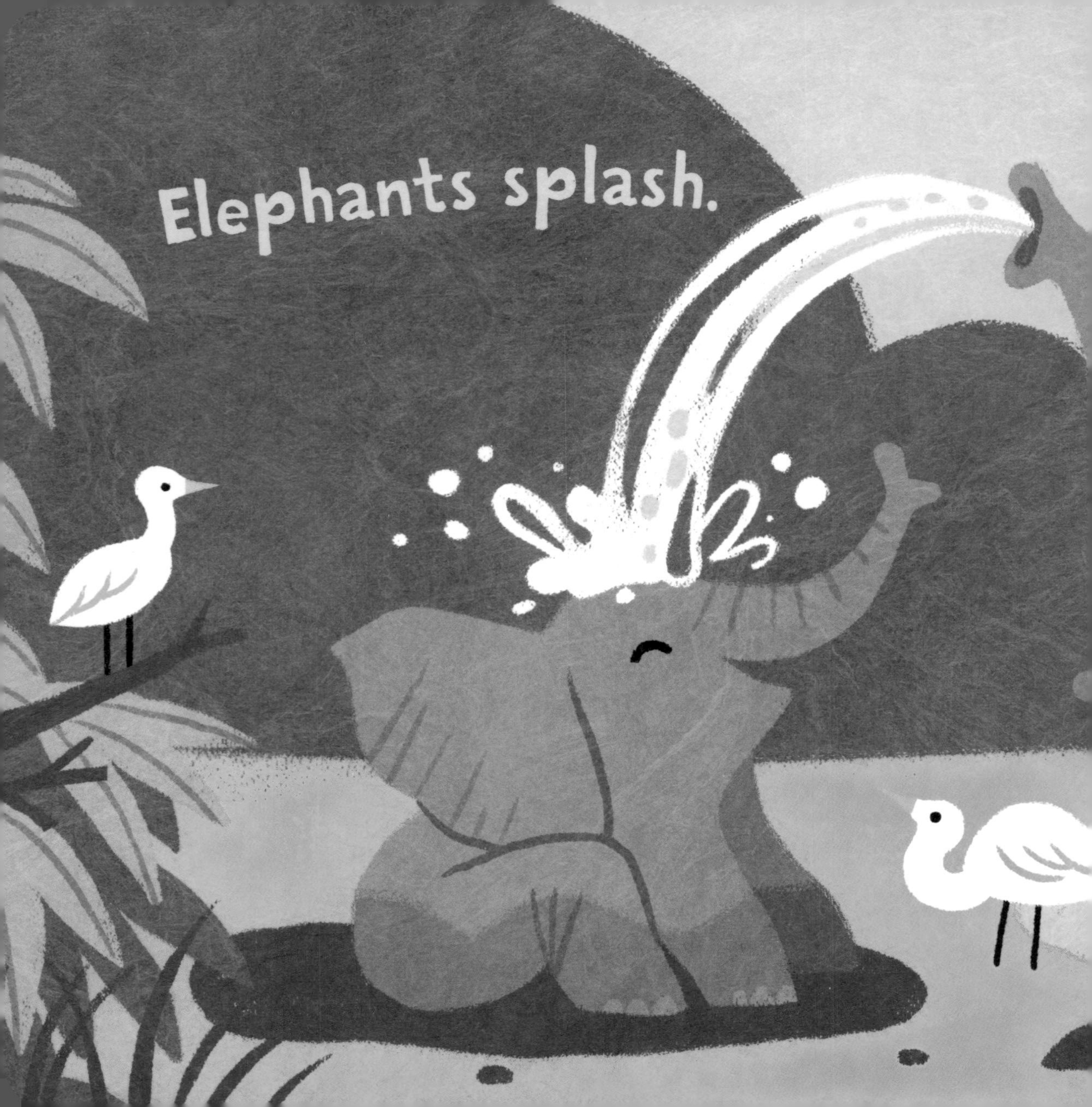

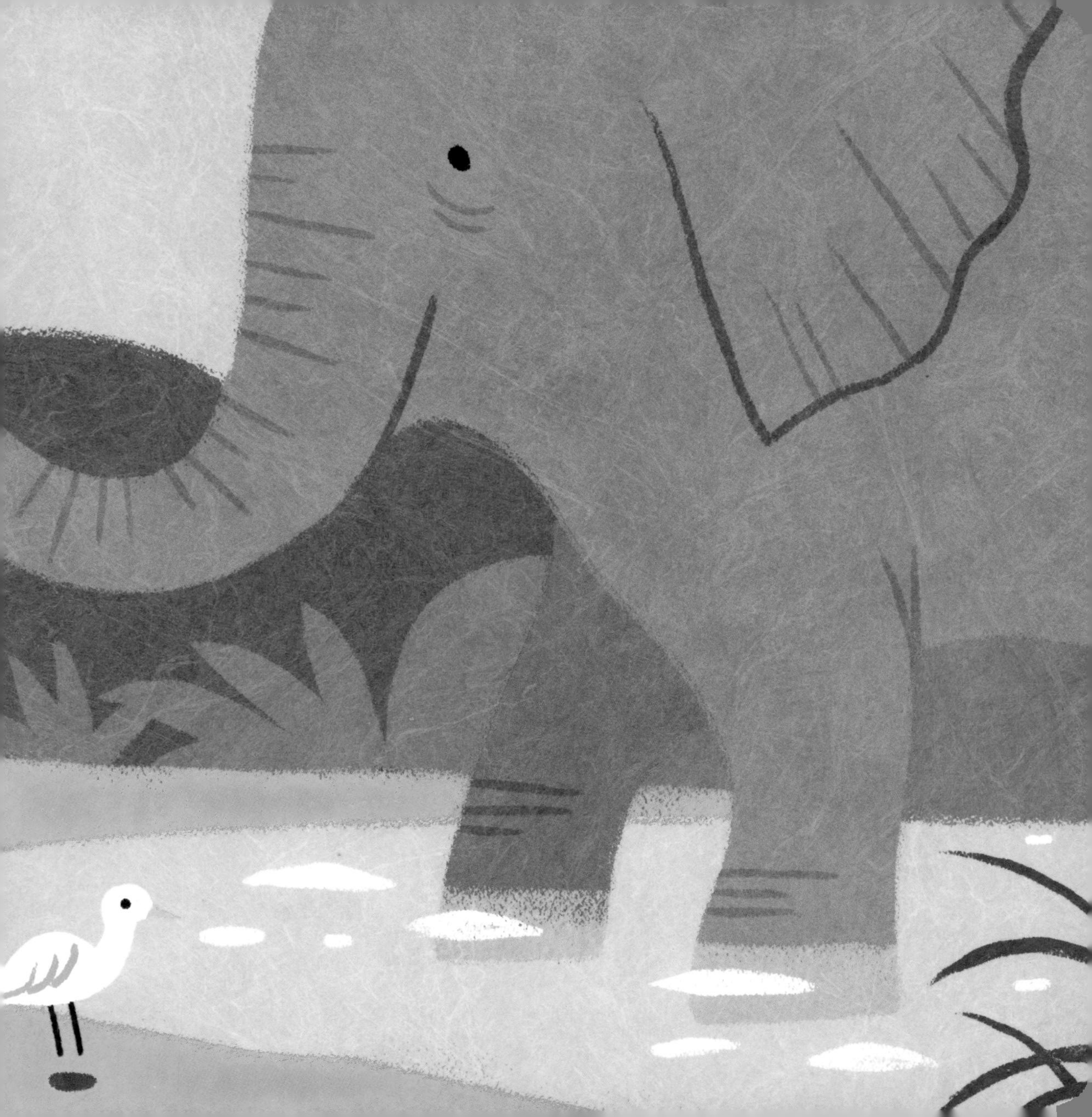

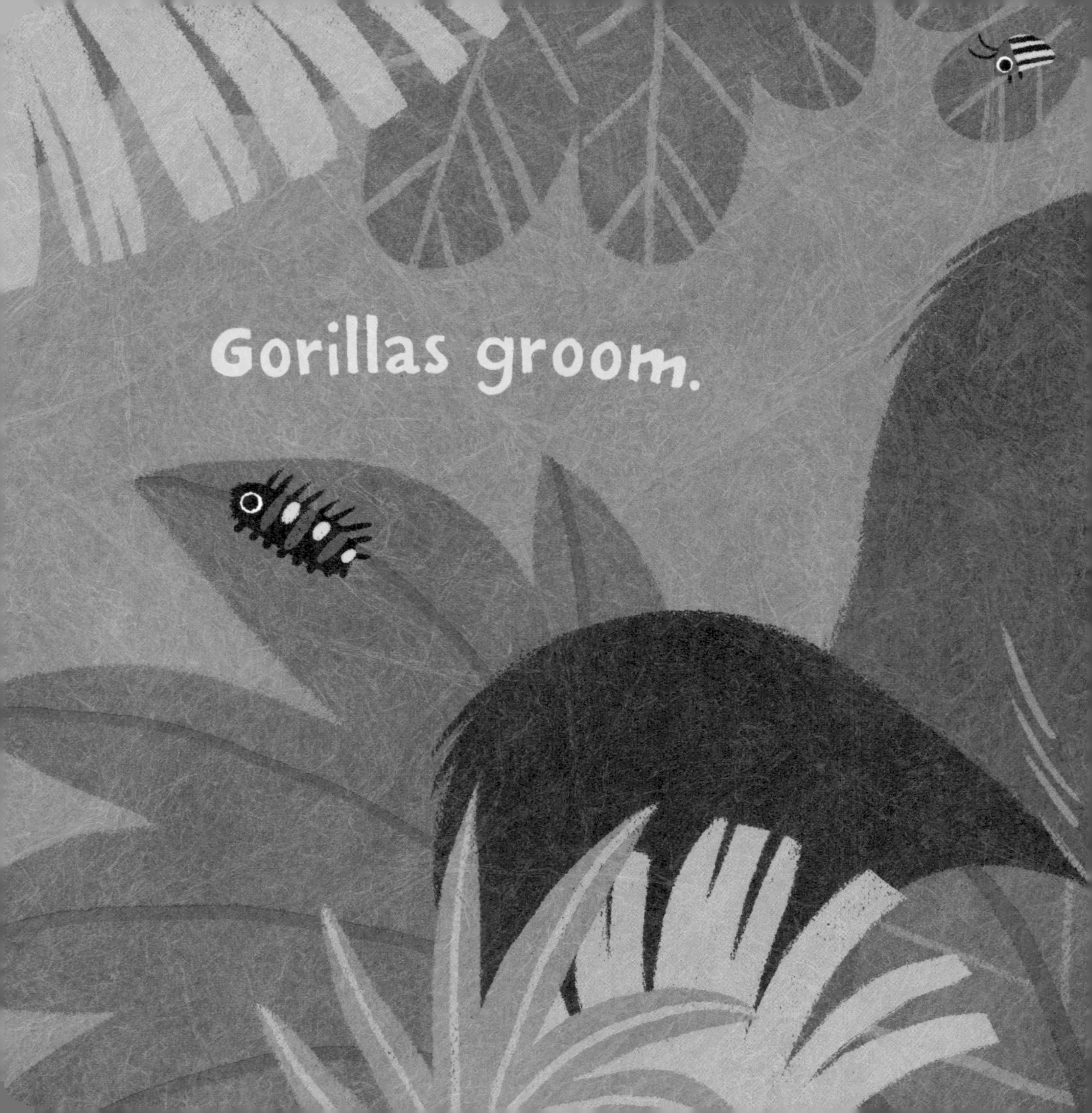

Gorillas groom.

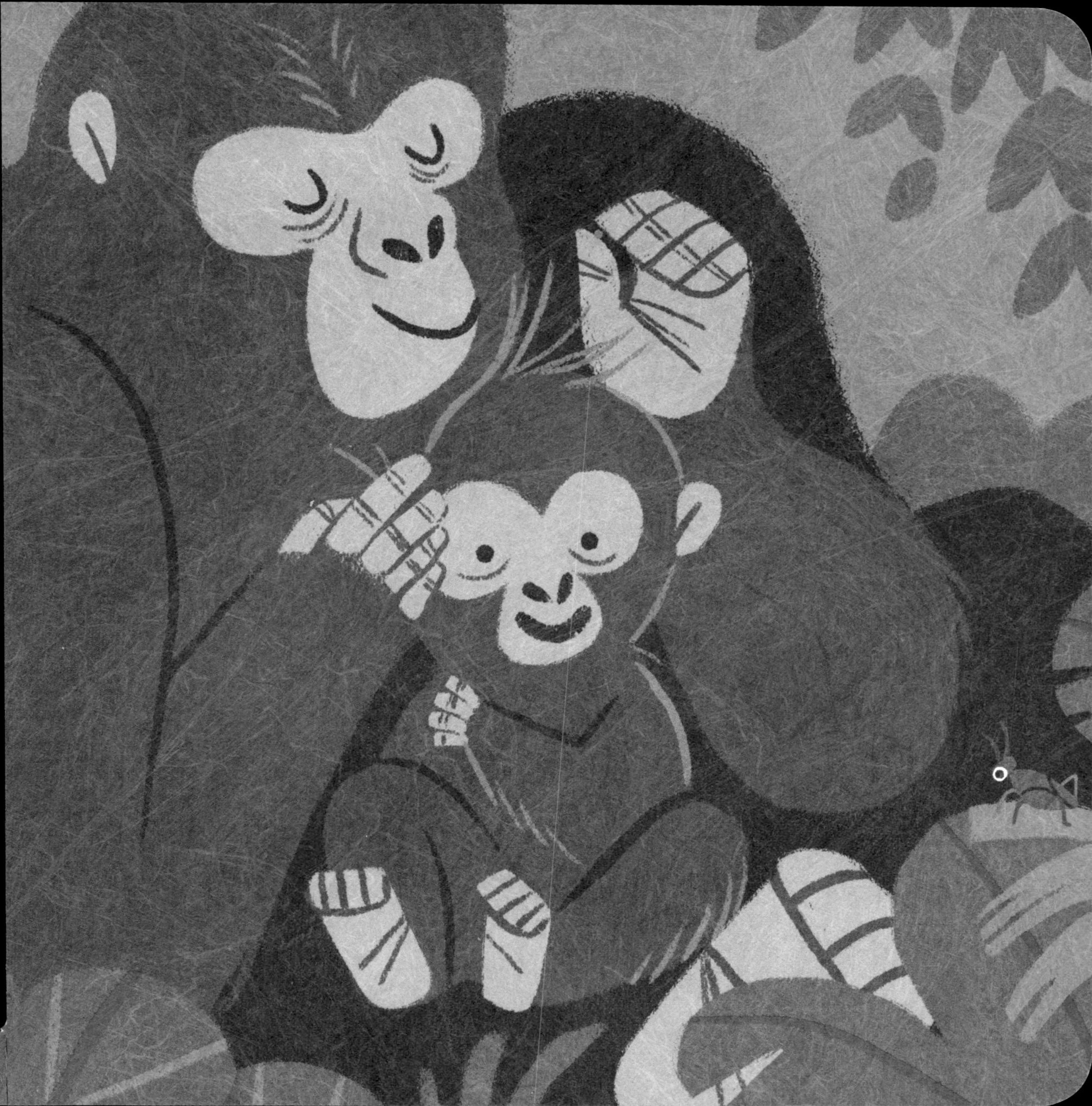

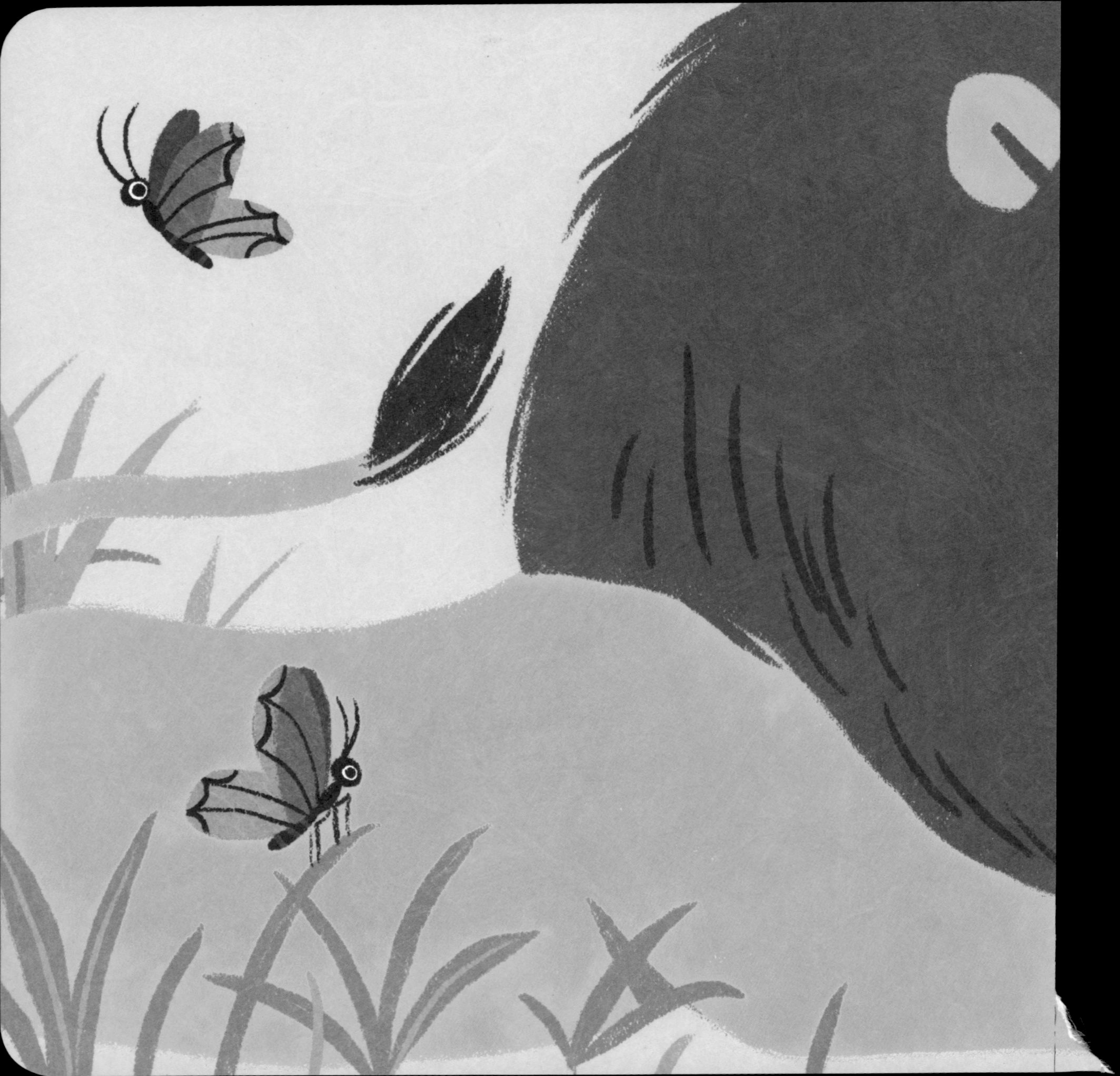

Lions lick their fur.

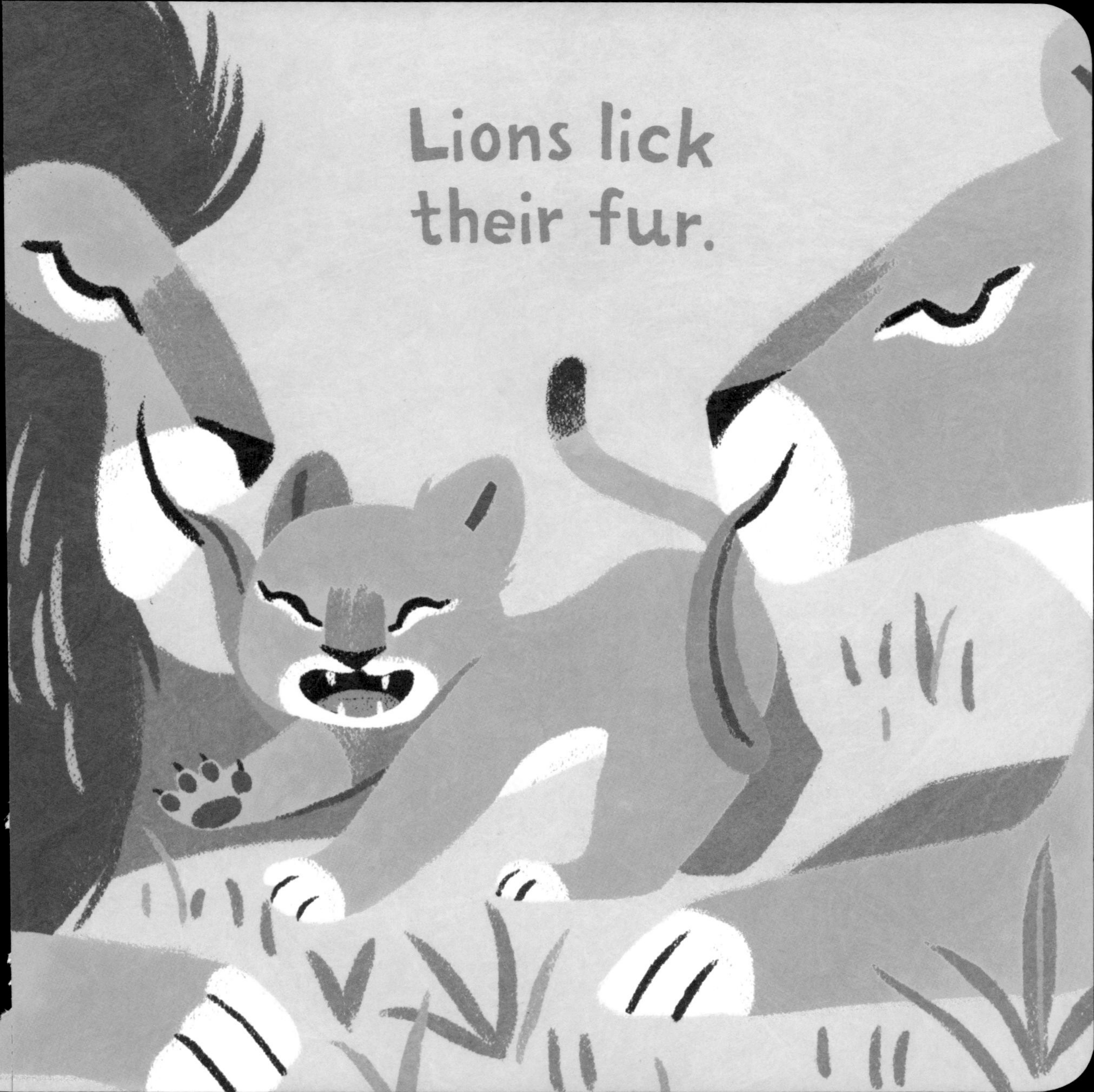

And babies like bubbles!

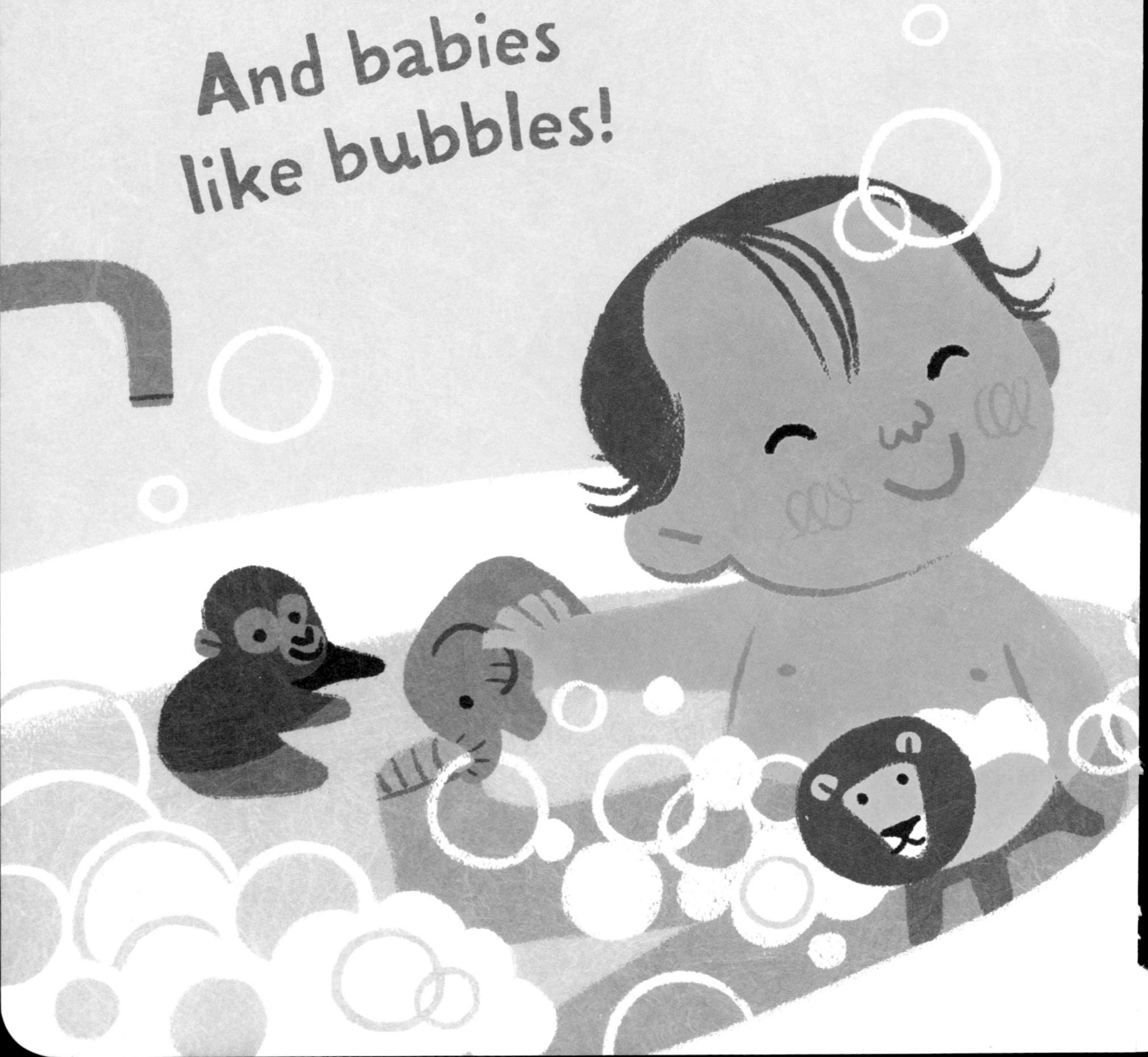